W9-BZU-291

Amazing Dogs

By Laura Buller

Penguin
Random
House

Series Editor Deborah Lock
US Senior Editor Shannon Beatty
Project Art Editor Hoa Luc
Art Director Martin Wilson
Producer, Pre-production Dragana Puvacic
Reading Consultant Linda Gambrell, Ph.D.

First American Edition, 2016
Published in the United States by DK Publishing
345 Hudson Street, New York, New York 10014

Copyright © 2016 Dorling Kindersley Limited
DK, a Division of Penguin Random House LLC
17 18 19 10 9 8 7 6 5 4
002—279719–July/2016

All rights reserved.
Without limiting the rights under copyright reserved above, no part of this publication may be
reproduced, stored in or introduced into a retrieval system, or transmitted, in any form, or by any
means (electronic, mechanical, photocopying, recording, or otherwise), without the prior written
permission of both the copyright owner and the above publisher of this book.
Published in Great Britain by Dorling Kindersley Limited.

A catalog record for this book is available from the Library of Congress.
ISBN: 978-1-4654-4596-4 (Paperback)
ISBN: 978-1-4654-4595-7 (Hardcover)

Printed in U.S.A.
DK books are available at special discounts when purchased in bulk for sales promotions, premiums,
fund-raising, or educational use. For details, contact: DK Publishing Special Markets, 345 Hudson
Street, New York, New York 10014 or SpecialSales@dk.com.

The publisher would like to thank the following for their kind permission to reproduce their photographs:
(Key: a-above; b-below/bottom; c-center; f-far; l-left; r-right; t-top)
1 Corbis: Kennan Harvey / Aurora Open. 6 Alamy Images: Kathy Hancock. 7 Corbis: 2 / MGP / Ocean (b);
Mark Edward Atkinson / Blend Images (tr). 8-9 Corbis: Denis Balibouse / Reuters. 10 Dreamstime.com: Ievgen
Melamud / Elmmksat (t). 11 Corbis: DK Limited (br); Russell Glenister (tr); Yoshihisa Fujita / MottoPet /
amanaimages (cla). 14 Corbis: Clive Chilvers / Demotix / Demotix / Demotix (cl). 14-15 Alamy Images: FEMA.
15 Alamy Images: Thorsten Eckert (tl). 18 Corbis: Renee DeMartin (cr). 18-19 Corbis: Tibor Bognar /
Photononstop. 19 Corbis: Radius Images (cr). 20 Alamy Images: Dave Porter (cl). 20-21 Corbis: Jack Affleck /
Aurora Open. 22 Dreamstime.com: Engin Korkmaz / Hypnocreative. 23 Dreamstime.com: Roughcollie. 24-25
Corbis: 68 / Ocean. 26 Corbis: Robert Dowling. 27 Alamy Images: Guenter, B. / Juniors Bildarchiv GmbH. 28
Alamy Images: Huntstock / Disability Images (bc). Corbis: Adie Bush / cultura (c). 29 Alamy Images: blickwinkel
/ Leithold (cr); tbkmedia.de (bc). Getty Images: Fuse (tr). 30 Corbis: Julian Smith / epa. 31 Corbis: Ali Abbas /
epa (bl); Radius Images (tr). 32 Alamy Images: blickwinkel / Schmidt-Roeger (tr). 32-33 Corbis: Penny Kendall /
Design Pics. 33 Corbis: Kennan Harvey / Aurora Open (bl). 34 Corbis: Olivier Maire / epa. 35 Corbis:
Jean-Christophe Bott / epa (bl); Alan Carey (cra). 38 Corbis: Frederic Larson / San Francisco Chronicle.
39 Corbis: Richard Hutchings. 40 Corbis: Brian Mitchell. 41 Corbis: Brian Mitchell (bl); Tom Nebbia (cra).
42 Alamy Images: AF archive (ca, c, bc).
Jacket images: Front: Corbis: Russell Glenister.Fotolia: fotojagodka (ca)
Back: Corbis: 2 / MGP / Ocean (tl)
All other images © Dorling Kindersley Limited
For further information see: www.dkimages.com

A WORLD OF IDEAS:
SEE ALL THERE IS TO KNOW
www.dk.com

Contents

Dogs from Small to Tall

Pekingese

Jack Russell terrier

Basset hound

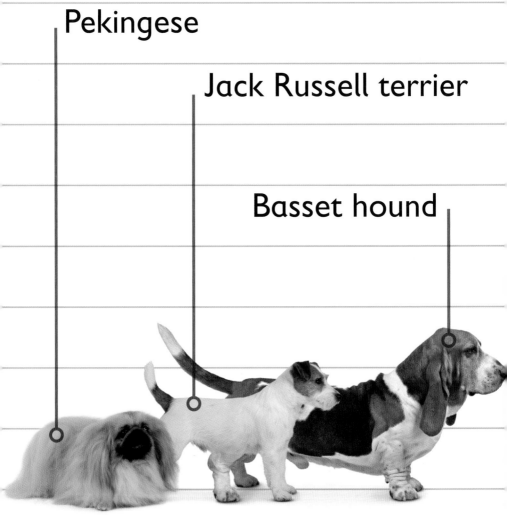

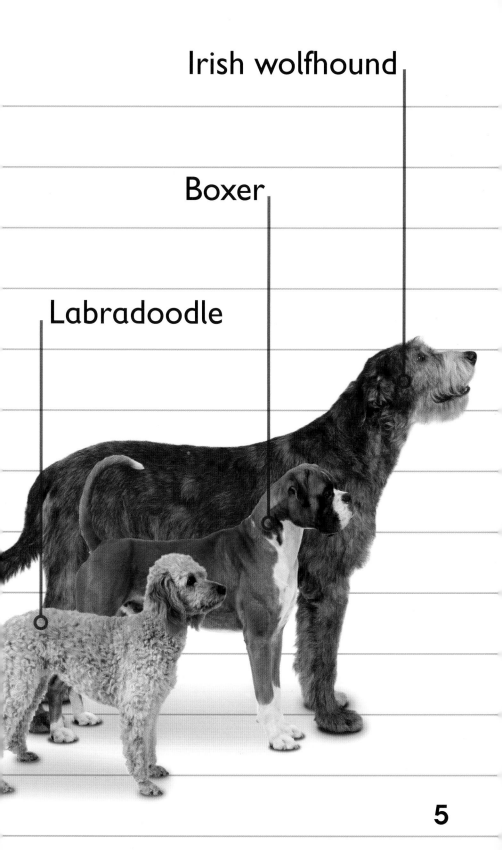

Irish wolfhound

Boxer

Labradoodle

5

CHAPTER 1
Hello, Doggy!

"Woof, woof!"

Dogs bark to say hello.

There are all kinds of dogs.
Some are very tiny.
You can pick
them up for
a cuddle. Other
dogs are very big.
You can hardly get your
arms around them for a hug!

Dogs belong to an animal family called **mammals**. They have fur, or hair, like all mammals. (You are a mammal, too!)

Baby dogs are called puppies. They drink milk from their mothers. Milk helps puppies grow bigger and stronger.

Puppy Games

Puppies love to play.

They need to go for walks and run around. This **exercise** helps them grow.

Puppies also
play to learn.

They learn how to get
along with other dogs.

CHAPTER 2
Super Senses

Dogs have super-strong **senses**. They can see better than you can—even in dim light.

They perk up their ears to hear sounds— even when you think it is quiet. But a dog's real superpower is its sense of smell.

Dogs have super senses and skills. What can they do with them? They can do lots of things!

Some dogs are really amazing. They do some amazing jobs.

SUPERDOG!

He hears faraway sounds
that humans cannot!
Never fear, Superdog
will hear.

He sees faraway things
that you'd never spot!
Even a flea, Superdog sees.

His smelling is telling him
just what is what!
He follows his nose,
wherever he goes.
That's **SUPERDOG!**

CHAPTER 3
Round Up !

How do farmers keep
their sheep safe?
They depend
on sheepdogs.

These dogs protect
the sheep from danger.
A sheepdog barks loudly
to scare away wild animals.
"Ruff! RUFF!"

How is a **herd** of **cattle** kept together? This is the job of a smart cattle dog.

This dog sees a cow stray from the herd. It nips the cow's ankle and the cow returns to the herd.

"Nip! Nip!"

Help Wanted!

Shepherd seeks a loyal and brave herding dog.

Do you know a dog that is fast on its feet and likes working in a team? Then this is the job for them!

The job:

- keeping bad animals away

- obeying whistles to gather sheep

- running at a steady and strong pace

Apply to:

Mr. Shep Herd

Woolly Woo Farm

Email: shep123@Woollywoofarm.com

CHAPTER 4
Pooch Power!

"Brrrrrrr!" It's freezing cold near the snowy **north pole**.

But this team of brave husky
dogs gets the job done.
They work together to pull
a heavy **sled**.

"Mush!" cries the driver,
as the dogs pull and pull.

This mountain dog is big and strong. Farmers use dogs like this to help with the jobs.

They hitch the dog to a wooden cart. The cart is loaded with milk, cheese, fruit, and vegetables. The dog pulls the cart to the market.

Home Help

How are these dogs being helpful?

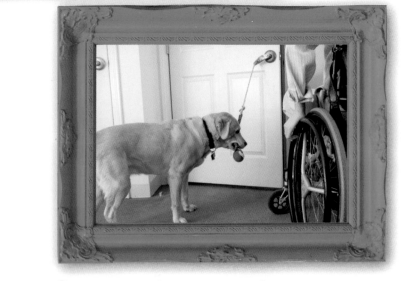

CHAPTER 5

Dogs on Duty

"Sniff! Sniff!" These dogs are not being nosy. They are using their keen sense of smell to help the police.

Police sniffer dogs do all kinds of useful work.

They can track down runaway prisoners.

They can sniff out bad things and sense danger.

"Help!" Someone is in trouble. Call in the **rescue** dogs!

A person may get lost or stuck, or be in danger. A rescue dog uses its sniffing skills to find the person. Then rescue workers can get the person out of trouble.

The most famous rescue dogs are Saint Bernards. They come from the snowy **Swiss Alps**.

Climbers may get buried in the snow. The dogs set off to find them. They dig through the snow.

Then they keep people warm until help arrives.

Rescue Training

Search and rescue dogs are trained to find people using one or more of these skills.

Air scent dog:
picks up a person's scent in the air.

Water search dog:
picks up a person's scent in or under the water.

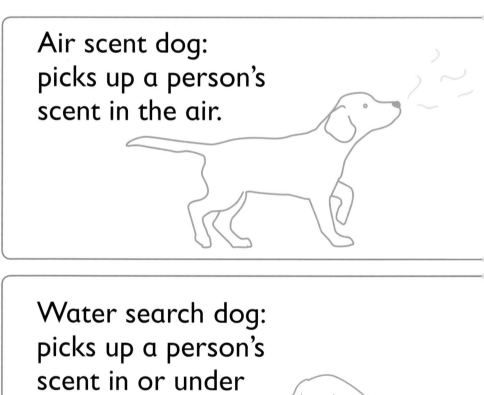

Trailing dog: follows a person's scent close to the ground.

Tracking dog: follows a person's path.

Avalanche dog: picks up a person's scent in or under snow.

CHAPTER 6
Helping Hounds

Some people need a little extra help. There's a smart dog to help!

Dogs help people who are unable to see, hear, or get around. These helpful dogs make jobs easier and safer for people.

Dogs can make people feel good. They are good friends for children with autism. Dogs make sick people cheerful. They are fun for lonely people.

Thank you, dogs, for all the amazing jobs you do!

FAMOUS DOGS

These dogs appear in books and films. They have amazing jobs, too!

Amazing Dogs Quiz

1. Where do Saint Bernards come from?

2. What is a dog's best sense?

3. How do cattle dogs keep cows in the herd?

4. What does the driver of a sled say to the husky dogs?

5. What animal family do dogs belong to?

Answers on page 45.

Glossary

cattle name for a group of cows

exercise activity that keeps a person or animal fit and healthy

herd group of animals that are the same

mammals group of animals, including humans, that have fur or hair, are warm-blooded, and have backbones

north pole most northern place on Earth

rescue save someone from a dangerous place or situation

senses five senses are sight, smell, hearing, taste, and touch

sled small vehicle on runners for travel over snow or ice

Swiss Alps area of mountains that crosses many countries in central Europe, including Switzerland

Answers to the Amazing Dogs Quiz:
1. The Swiss Alps; **2**. Its sense of smell; **3**. Dogs nip the cows on their ankles; **4**. Mush!; **5**. Dogs are mammals.

Guide for Parents

DK Readers is a four-level interactive reading adventure series for children, developing the habit of reading widely for both pleasure and information. These books have an exciting main narrative interspersed with a range of reading genres to suit your child's reading ability. Each book is designed to develop your child's reading skills, fluency, grammar awareness, and comprehension in order to build confidence and engagement when reading.

Ready for a *Beginning to Read* book

YOUR CHILD SHOULD

- be familiar with using beginning letter sounds and context clues to figure out unfamiliar words.
- be aware of the need for a slight pause at commas and a longer one at periods.
- alter his/her expression for questions and exclamations.

A VALUABLE AND SHARED READING EXPERIENCE

For many children, reading requires much effort, but adult participation can make this both fun and easier. So here are a few tips on how to use this book with your child.

TIP 1 Check out the contents together before your child begins:

- read the text about the book on the back cover.
- flip through the book and stop to chat about the contents page together to heighten your child's interest and expectation.
- make use of unfamiliar or difficult words on the page in a brief discussion.
- chat about the nonfiction reading features used in the book, such as headings, captions, recipes, lists, or charts.

TIP 2 Support your child as he/she reads the story pages:

- give the book to your child to read and turn the pages.
- where necessary, encourage your child to break a word into syllables, sound out each one, and then flow the syllables together. Ask him/her to reread the sentence to check the meaning.
- when there's a question mark or an exclamation mark, encourage your child to vary his/her voice as he/she reads the sentence. Demonstrate how to do this if it is helpful.

TIP 3 Chat at the end of each page:

- the factual pages tend to be more difficult than the story pages, and are designed to be shared with your child.
- ask questions about the text and the meaning of the words used. These help to develop comprehension skills and awareness of the language used.

A FEW ADDITIONAL TIPS

- Always encourage your child to try reading difficult words by themselves. Praise any self-corrections, for example, "I like the way you sounded out that word and then changed the way you said it, to make sense."
- Try to read together everyday. Reading little and often is best. These books are divided into manageable chapters for one reading session. However, after 10 minutes, only keep going if your child wants to read on.
- Read other books of different types to your child just for enjoyment and information.

Series consultant, **Dr. Linda Gambrell**, Distinguished Professor of Education at Clemson University, has served as President of the National Reading Conference, the College Reading Association, and the International Reading Association.

Index